Little Pebble™

Mammals in the Wild

Seals

A 4D BOOK

by Kathryn Clay

PEBBLE
a capstone imprint

Download the Capstone 4D app!

- Ask an adult to download the Capstone 4D app.

- Scan the cover and stars inside the book for additional content.

When you scan a spread, you'll find fun extra stuff to go with this book! You can also find these things on the web at www.capstone4D.com using the password: seals.00788

Pebble Books are published by Pebble
1710 Roe Crest Drive, North Mankato,
Minnesota 56003
www.mycapstone.com

Library of Congress Cataloging-in-Publication Data
Names: Clay, Kathryn, author.
Title: Seals : a 4D book / by Kathryn Clay.
Description: North Mankato, Minnesota : an imprint of
    Pebble, [2019] | Series: Little Pebble. Mammals in the
    wild | Audience: Age 4-7.
Identifiers: LCCN 2018004132 (print) | LCCN 2018009135
    (ebook) | ISBN 9781977100900 (eBook PDF) | ISBN
    9781977100788 (hardcover) | ISBN 9781977100849
    (paperback)
Subjects: LCSH: Seals—Juvenile literature.
Classification: LCC QL737.P6 (ebook) | LCC QL737.P6
    C53 2019 (print) | DDC 599.79—dc23
LC record available at https://lccn.loc.gov/2018004132

Editorial Credits
Karen Aleo, editor; Juliette Peters, designer;
Tracy Cummins and Heather Mauldin, media researchers;
Laura Manthe, production specialist

Photo Credits
Getty Images: Doug Lindstrand, 9; iStockphoto: Focus_
on_Nature, 13, Onfokus, 21; Shutterstock: AKKHARAT
JARUSILAWONG, 7, Aleksei Potov, Cover, critterbiz, 11,
FloridaStock, 19, Ian Dyball, 17, Judith Lienert, 15, Nattle,
Design Element, Randy Bjorklund, 1, SAPhotog, 5

Printed in the United States of America.
PA021

Table of Contents

At Sea

Bark! Bark!

A seal swims close by.

Brrr. Seals live in cold water.

They have blubber and fur.

Both keep them warm.

Seals swim fast.

They have four flippers.

Flippers help them

swim and turn.

flippers

See the long whiskers?

They help to find fish.

Chomp!

Seals are mammals.

They hold their breath

in the water.

They come up to breathe.

On Land

Seals rest on ice or land.

The sun warms them.

15

Some seals live alone.

Others live in groups.

A group of seals is
a colony.

Baby harp seals are white.

Other seals are gray, black,

or brown.

baby harp seal

Baby Seals

Pups are born on land.

They drink milk.

Soon they will eat fish.

Glossary

blubber—a thick layer of fat under the skin of some animals; blubber keeps animals warm

colony—a group of the same kind of animal

flipper—one of the broad, flat limbs of a sea creature

mammal—a warm-blooded animal that breathes air; mammals have hair or fur; female mammals feed milk to their young

pup—a young seal

whisker—a long, stiff hair growing on the face and bodies of some animals

Read More

Beltran, Roxanne, and Patrick Robinson. *A Seal Named Patches.* Fairbanks, Alaska: University of Alaska Press, 2017.

Gregory, Josh. *Seals.* Nature's Children. New York: Children's Press, an imprint of Scholastic, Inc., 2015.

Hodgkins, Fran. *Do Seals Ever . . .?: Sea Lions, Walruses, and Manatees.* Camden, Maine: Down East, 2017.

Internet Sites

Use FactHound to find Internet sites related to this book.

Visit www.facthound.com

Just type in 9781977100788 and go.

Super-cool stuff! Check out projects, games and lots more at **www.capstonekids.com**

Critical Thinking Questions

1. How do seals use their flippers?

2. What do seals eat?

3. How do seals breathe?

Index